TRUCK CARGO

Transportation and Trade Series

by

June Behrens

photographs collected by

Lou Jacobs Jr.

AN ELK GROVE BOOK

 CHILDRENS PRESS, CHICAGO

The author wishes to thank Robert L. McHale
of the AMERICAN TRUCKING ASSOCIATIONS,
INC., for his cooperation in supplying source materials
and references used in the preparation of this book.

CONTENTS

THE NATION'S MARKETPLACE

A big moving van stopped down the street today. Soon we will meet our new neighbors. They are one of every five families in the United States who will move to a new neighborhood this year. Their household goods were brought from the midwest on a long haul drive by a tractor-trailer moving van.

We often see moving vans in our neighborhood and delivery trucks in our community. On the highways we pass the long tractor-trailer rigs, moving goods to another city or state. One in every six motor vehicles on the road is a truck, serving the transportation needs of our community, state and nation.

Trucking is big business, an industry second only to agriculture in the United States. The trucking industry employs over ten million people, contributing almost 11% to our nation's total wealth and economy.

Trucks and the Nation's economy. Everything we eat, wear or use is brought at least part way by truck. Our national economy depends upon trucks to carry the cargo to all our population, in the smallest towns and the largest cities.

Trucks follow the roads that link the most distant marketplaces to our nation of cities. There are almost 36,000 communities in the United States which depend on the trucking industry, having no transportation other than automobiles to serve their economic needs.

The production of our factories and farms depends upon distribution. Trucks go anywhere a highway or a road goes. Trucks bring together the production-processing-distribution pattern of our economy.

Changing a way of life. The trucking industry has helped to make our lives better. Within the past fifty years there have been changes in our eating habits. There have been changes in cities and suburbs and changes in manufacturing and farming. There have been changes in education. How has trucking helped to bring about these changes?

Trucks have helped to mechanize and modernize farming methods, resulting in the greater production needed to feed our growing nation.

No matter where we live we can enjoy "seasonal" foods all year around. Fast refrigerator trucks speed fresh fruits and vegetables from the winter marketplaces in the United States to cold climate states.

Many people have moved from crowded cities to suburbs where mills and factories have been built. It is no longer necessary to build one big factory in a great industrial center.

Little factories built in city suburbs depend on trucking to get their products to a central assembly plant. These new factories bring economic growth to the communities.

At one time factory locations were dependent upon the raw materials available as well as rail or water transportation for the distribution of goods. Today factories are built nearer to the markets. Trucks provide the transportation needed by industry.

Busing has brought rural schools into larger school districts, improving the quality of education. Bookmobiles, traveling museums and other exhibits on wheels have helped to increase our knowledge.

The trucking industry has helped to change and improve our way of life.

WHAT IS TRUCK CARGO?

Nearly everything that is manufactured, grown or mined from the earth is carried by truck. Nearly everything that is moved in trade or commerce by air, sea or rail has been brought part way as truck cargo.

Anything that can be moved from one place to another is cargo. One trucking company sign reads, "We haul anything that is loose at both ends."

Moving cargo by truck is the most widely used means of transporting goods. It is limited only by the more than three million miles of highways in our nation. Where there is a road, there is a truck route. Movement of cargo by sea, rail and air is limited to waterways, railways and airports.

Intermodal cargo. Trucking is a means or mode of transportation, just as trains and ships are modes of transportation. When cargo travels by more than one mode it is called intermodal cargo.

The trucking industry often works in cooperation with sea, rail and air facilities, providing economical benefits to the public. It is an advantage to the consumer for each mode to work in cooperation with the other.

Containerizing cargo. A cargo container may be the van or enclosed part of the truck bed. It may be a refrigerated box, a tank, a car carrier or a dry bulk carrier. Some containers are collapsible and expandable.

Demountable cargo containers can be lifted off the body or frame of the truck or trailer. The most commonly used size is eight feet high, eight feet wide and from ten to forty feet long.

Cargo carried in demountable containers can be moved from one mode of transportation to another. The containers then become intermodal cargo.

Piggyback. Containerized cargo on trucks and trailers sometimes travels piggyback. This is the term used when the containers are lifted off the truck frame, or trailers are detached from the tractor, and loaded onto railroad flatcars. Piggyback transportation is used when it proves more economical and efficient for the shipper over a long haul.

Fishyback. Containerized cargo arrives by ship from another port. A traveling gantry crane lifts the container from the deck of the ship and loads it onto a waiting truck frame. The cargo has traveled fishyback, from truck to ship to truck again, then direct to your city or town.

Containerized cargo traveling by fishyback remains sealed. Handling costs are reduced and cargo damage is light.

Birdyback. When cargo travels part of the way on its journey by aircraft, it is called birdyback cargo.

Intermodal cargo shipment. A good example of the use of intermodal transportation is the movement of a trailer load of frozen foods bound for Alaska.

The refrigerated containerized cargo is lifted from the truck frame onto a ship in Seattle. The refrigerator unit is plugged into the ship's power, maintaining the temperature. At Anchorage, Alaska, the container is lifted from the ship onto a railroad flatcar and plugged into the train power. At Fairbanks, Alaska, the containerized frozen foods are placed on a truck frame and delivered to the local supermarkets.

International cargo. When a trucking operation is carried on in two or more nations, it is called international trucking. Intermodal transportation encourages growth in international trucking. Some trucking companies in the United States have extended their service to other countries. This trailer is being towed to dock at Avonmouth, England.

HISTORY OF TRUCK CARGO

For over 150 years the old Conestoga wagon moved cargo westward in the building of a new nation. It might be called the ancestor of today's truck. The early wagon trains were cargo carriers, ushering in an arm of nation-wide transportation.

Horseless buggies. At the turn of the century, in 1893, horseless buggies or motor wagons were introduced and a year later the federal government bought three motorized delivery trucks. The Post Office was one of the first government agencies to use them.

Trucks did not become immediately popular. Bad roads limited their use. It was almost twenty years later, during World War I, that truck transportation came into its own.

World War I. Railroads were overworked and could not handle all the freight and cargo business created by the war. Thirty thousand trucks were ordered by the government to transport needed supplies. The trucks proved their worth. They could go anywhere there was a road, to markets not reached by train.

Federal Laws. In 1916, the Federal Road Aid Act was passed, providing federal aid to states for road building. By the end of the war there were 300,000 miles of surfaced roads and thousands of surplus trucks.

The Federal Highway Act of 1921, worked out the first United States highway system. Business, agriculture and industry saw the value of trucking as a means of economical, reliable transportation.

World War II. World War II gave trucking another spurt of growth. Trucking provided needed, flexible transportation in a time of emergency.

GROWTH OF TRUCK CARGO SERVICE

Today more than sixteen million trucks move cargo across our nation. Our economy depends on trucking, which has grown to be our second largest industry.

The growth of truck cargo transportation would not have been possible without the road building and highway construction programs.

The highway system linked cities in our nation to each other, then rural America to the cities. Trucking traveled the highways to growth and expansion.

5143

N Y 6 224358 T M T

68 NEVADA 33031 M C 69 NEVADA

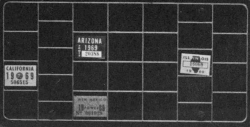

ARIZONA 1969 20388

CALIFORNIA 19 69 506515

ILLINOIS 16968 1969

NEW MEXICO SE 661025

69 WYOMING PSC 6 4354 PERMIT

MISSISSIPPI 21333 OCT. PUB. SER. COM. 69

R. R. COMM. A5803 68 TEXAS 69

KCC 1968 4165

The user tax. Over three million miles of all-weather surfaced roads have been built from user tax. A user tax is paid by the user of the highway as he drives. He is taxed for the gasoline he uses, for license plates and licenses. Trucks must be licensed in each state they carry goods. One truck may have many license plates.

The user pays tax on new trucks, automobiles and parts. He pays tolls on ferries and roads. This tax money helps build new roads and repair old ones.

The National System of Interstate and Defense Highways, to be completed in 1972, consists of over 41,000 miles of super highways covering 49 states and linking every city with a population of over 50,000. This project has been in progress since 1956. It is being paid by Federal and state user taxes.

Trucking rules and regulations. When the economy of the country depends upon an industry for growth and progress, it becomes necessary for the states and the Federal government to establish certain rules or regulations.

These rules are made to protect the interests of the public as well as the trucking industry.

There are regulations on carrier rates charged and on kinds of cargo the trucks may haul. There are rules governing the routes and roads the trucks may travel.

Each state sets up limits on the weight trucks may carry over their highways as well as the size and lengths of trucks. States post speed limits for trucks.

When trucks move over state lines, their travel becomes interstate. Federal rules are established by the Interstate Commerce Commission. The letters ICC on a truck mean the cargo carrier operates under Interstate Commerce Commission regulations. The ICC regulates commerce among the states and enforces strict safety rules.

Future growth: Giants. Truck-trains on super highways may be a part of the future. Truck tractors hauling three trailers with a total length of over 103 feet have seen limited use. The truck-train drivers call them "triple bottom" rigs.

The future of trucking may see jet powered cargo carriers, controlled by computers, truly giants of the highway.

KINDS OF CARGO CARRIERS

Classes of trucks. Trucks are generally classified as "private" carriers or "for-hire" carriers.

Private truck operators (merchants, manufacturers, etc.) are shippers who carry their own goods in their own trucks. The Interstate Commerce Commission has no authority over these truckers other than enforcement of safety regulations.

For-hire carriers haul the goods or cargo of others for a fee. For-hire carriers may include city, state and interstate trucking companies.

For-hire contract carriers haul cargo for certain shippers only, under a written agreement or contract. For-hire common carriers haul goods for any shipper.

Truck body types. Straight trucks have the engine, cab and cargo space mounted on the same body or frame. Straight trucks include panel bodies, pickup trucks, vans, flat-bed and stake trucks.

The dump truck is a straight truck with a body that can be tilted to empty its load. Straight trucks range in size from the smallest panel truck to a large transport carrier.

The tractor-trailer rig (rig means equipment) is made up of parts. The tractor houses the cab and the engine or power unit and does the pulling. The semi-trailer or trailer carries the cargo. The semi-trailer has back wheels and the front hitches onto the tractor. The full trailer has wheels on both front and back.

A "combination" is the straight truck or tractor coupled to a trailer.

The double bottom or twin trailer unit consists of the tractor, semi-trailer and full trailer combination.

Truck engines. Trucks and tractor-trailer combinations burn either gasoline or diesel fuel.

Long haul trucks and tractor-trailer rigs that travel cross-country are usually powered by diesel engines. They burn diesel oil fuel, cutting down on operating costs. Diesel trucks usually have an exhaust pipe that sticks up above the cab.

Trucks operating with gasoline engines are most often used in cities and towns or on short haul runs.

Trucks used in community service. Some trucks are owned and maintained by our cities. They do a public service in keeping our communities safe and clean. They include garbage trucks, fire trucks, street sweepers, street repair and maintenance trucks.

Other trucks bring many conveniences to our homes. The milk truck, delivery trucks from city merchants, the bakery truck, or service repair trucks, all help to make our lives more comfortable. Moving vans make the job of moving easier for families.

The school bus transports children, who sometime might go to school in a mobile classroom trailer. Children in some areas check out books from the bookmobile, which is a walk-through truck van. They might visit a traveling museum or get a periodic checkup from the X-ray lab on wheels. All are a part of the truck family, serving the needs of our community.

Cargo trucks for farming. Pickup and flat-bed trucks are the two all-purpose trucks used by the farmer. Specialist farmers need special kinds of trucking equipment.

The poultry producer depends upon the "cackle crate" carrier to haul his live poultry. Temperature controlled panel trucks are used for egg shipments.

Cattlemen use the big semi-trailer livestock rigs capable of carrying forty head of cattle. Some have sprinkling systems to cool off the livestock during travel time.

Dairymen depend upon temperature controlled tank trucks for their milk shipments.

Grain farmers use dry bulk carriers and flat bed grain body trucks to deliver their product to the mill.

Fresh produce requires a controlled temperature to reach distant marketplaces in good condition. The produce farmer uses refrigerated trucks and trailers to haul his perishable foods.

Trucks used in construction. Heavy equipment carriers are low-bed heavy haulers which carry bulldozers, scrapers and other construction equipment. The dump truck may be a body of any type or size. Agitator body trucks mix concrete on the way to the job.

Trucks in manufacturing and industry. Whatever the cargo, there is a truck to fill the need. Tractor-trailer rigs haul the raw material and finished product. Tank trucks carry liquid and bulk. Flat beds are used for lumber and packaged and containerized cargo. Vans are all-utility carriers.

Trucks for natural resources. Log body trucks are built specially for transporting logs. The trailer body has support bars instead of a bed. The logs are stacked on the support bars and chained into place.

Oilfield body trucks have a platform body and carry equipment for oil drilling. These trucks are often used in the field, where there are no constructed roads.

Special carriers are required for mining coal and other minerals. These heavy hauler and dump trucks are working a two mile wide copper mine near Salt Lake City, Utah.

Trucks used for special purposes. Armored trucks are money carriers. They are especially constructed of heavy armor to protect their cargo.

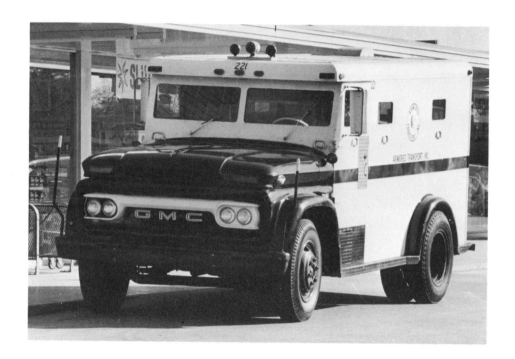

Auto transports are carriers built to haul as many as nine automobiles from the assembly plant to the automobile agency.

The missile carrier consists of a flat bed truck body which has been built to carry rockets and other cargo of great length. Manufacturers can assemble the structure in the plant and it is then sent to the launch pad by missile carrier.

"Cherry pickers" are trucks with a movable tower or boom. At the top of the tower is a small enclosed platform capable of holding one or two men. The cherry picker is used to raise workmen to great heights for tree trimming, changing street lights and signs. One of the tallest cherry pickers is used to pluck the astronauts from the space capsule when it is on the launching pad.

Campers and house trailers are trucks used for recreation. Some people in the community live in house trailers as their permanent homes.

THE TRUCK DRIVER: KNIGHT OF THE ROAD

Have you ever been to a roadeo? The roadeo is a nationwide contest for truck drivers, testing their driving ability. Drivers from all over the United States meet to compete for the national championship award. It is a great honor to win the roadeo.

Trucking companies sponsor contests and award prizes to drivers in their company for safety driver records and courtesy on the road. This recognition to drivers helps to make everyone aware of their important jobs.

Drivers are professionals. Many go to training schools to learn how to handle special trucking equipment. Drivers, who cross state lines, called interstate drivers, know the traffic rules for each state. They must learn the Interstate Commerce Commission regulations. Long haul road drivers pass strict physical examinations every six months.

Truck drivers are skilled and well trained workers who contribute much to our nation's welfare and economy.

Over the road drivers. The over the road or long haul road drivers usually operate the gasoline or diesel powered tractor-trailers. They deliver goods over long distances and spend most of their time driving. They are also called intercity or interstate line haul drivers, trucking from one city or state to another over a specific route or line.

On long trips companies sometimes send out two drivers. These drivers work as a team. One drives while the other rests or sleeps. There is a bunk behind the air-conditioned cab, with a comfortable foam rubber mattress. The drivers trade off after a certain number of hours or miles.

Over the road drivers keep records in a log book. Drivers must record every detail of their trip in the log book.

Local truck drivers. Local drivers are assigned to make pick-ups and deliveries from a central terminal or warehouse. They transport goods locally from warehouses, cargo terminals and factories to wholesalers, retailers and consumers. They operate big trucks as well as tractor-trailers and must maneuver them on city streets.

Local drivers handle delivery forms, cargo bills and sometimes collect money. Their trucks may be loaded when they start a run, or they might help with the loading and unloading at pick-up and delivery points.

Routemen. The routeman is part salesman and part driver. Routemen generally drive light trucks over a regular route, delivering goods and selling or providing services. Drivers who deliver directly to the public are called retail routemen, such as the drycleaner. The wholesale routeman is the driver who makes deliveries of dairy and food products to markets.

THE TRUCK CARGO TERMINAL

The truck cargo terminal might be called the "nerve center" of all cargo movement. It is the traffic control center which schedules the movement of every incoming and outgoing cargo item. Terminal activity controls the movements of the fleets of trucks delivering and receiving cargo.

Terminal directors. The terminal Director of Operations and his men are in charge of all trucking movements, local as well as long haul, between cities and terminals. Dispatchers keep in touch with drivers on the road by two way radio telephone.

Dispatchers, cargo handlers, dock workers and warehousemen work with the Director of Operations in moving the cargo shipments through the terminal.

The Maintenance Department keeps the fleet of trucks and trailers rolling. Mechanics keep the trucks in good running condition and maintain safety checks on all trucking equipment, which is serviced and inspected regularly.

The Traffic Control Department sets the prices for cargo delivery service. Charges for cargo handling are determined by the type of cargo, its weight and value as well as the distance it is to be shipped.

Cargo movements. The truck terminal never closes. It is an around the clock operation.

The terminal dock is the platform where trucks are loaded and unloaded. Incoming trucks, tractors and trailers back up to the docks in areas assigned to arriving cargo shipments.

One side of the dock may handle long distance hauls while the other side is used for local or city truck pickup and delivery.

Dispatchers know the arrival and departure time of all cargo and carriers. When an incoming long haul truck backs up to the dock, the central control room or dispatching office goes into operation to get the cargo to its final destination.

Cargo or freight handlers and fork lift operators unload the cargo and sort it, according to its destination, into conveyor carts. Cargo is carried by an automatic conveyor cart around the terminal dock to the outgoing shipment area.

Cargo is unloaded from the conveyor carts by the freight handlers into waiting trucks for local or over the road delivery. This method of unloading and reloading for distribution is called "progressive unloading."

Dock checkers and foremen count and supervise the transfer of cargo items being loaded for outbound delivery against the bills of lading. The bill of lading is an itemized bill of goods contained in a shipment.

The paperwork for each shipment—billing, scheduling, dispatching—is handled by the central control room.

When a local carrier brings cargo to the terminal, the driver gives the dispatcher an itemized list of goods in his shipment. The cargo is assigned to the line haul trucks according to its destination. The checker records the number of the outbound trailer on the bill of lading and the cargo leaves as soon as it is loaded.

Paperwork and billing for the shipment is handled by rate clerks in traffic control and telephoned to the receiving cargo terminal. This method of operation saves time and speeds cargo delivery.

ALL KINDS OF CARGO

Cargo might be perishable, live, wet, dry, hot, cold, solid, liquid, heavy, light, raw material or manufactured goods. Cargo is almost anything.

Certain chemicals and blood plasma are perishable cargo. Fruits and vegetables, fish, meat and frozen food are also perishables and require temperature controlled carriers.

Live cargo includes experimental rats for laboratory work, the "cackle crate" with its load of chickens, livestock of all kinds, school buses. All carry live cargo!

A tanker load of cherries is shipped in juice. A cement mixer works on the way to a construction job. Both are wet cargo.

Grains are dry cargo. Grains can be loaded into a dry bulk tanker trailer or sacked and stacked in flat bed trucks.

Steel girders for construction and gold bricks in an armored car are solid cargo; while tank trucks carrying milk, gasoline, vegetable oils and molasses are liquid cargo.

Raw material goes to the manufacturer and finished goods go to the consumer. All are cargo.

Mail cargo. Trucks have made many changes in mail service and delivery in the United States. Railroads and airplanes share the task of the longer hauls and trucks are the carriers on final delivery routes.

This rapid transportation gets our mail to us almost overnight, a few days at most from anywhere in the United States.

One of the longest mail truck deliveries is from Seattle, Washington, to Anchorage and Fairbanks, Alaska. Big tractors and trailers travel the 2000-mile Alcan Highway (much of it is gravel) to deliver packages. This mail run takes 96 hours. Letters go by air. When winter roads are not passable, the trucks go piggyback and fishyback. Trucking the mail has proven much faster than hauling by ship or rail.

Cargo requiring special handling. A missile base needs liquid oxygen at a temperature of 423 degrees F. *below* zero. Truck carriers meet the need by supplying a giant stainless steel vacuum bottle on wheels which will maintain the below zero temperature.

Hot asphalt is used in construction. It travels in an insulated trailer, 400 degrees F. *above* zero, ready for immediate use.

Space capsules and rocket motors, pillars for a sport stadium
and steel girders for bridges, all are cargo requiring special
handling.

Transportation is by heavy equipment carriers. The routes over which these carriers travel are carefully checked. Permission must be granted by the states where travel will take place.

In the past, the manufacturer of chocolate made his product, let it harden, packaged it in boxes and shipped it off to the candy factories. At the candy factories the chocolate was removed from the packaging, and remelted before use in the recipes for chocolate bars.

Today the chocolate is given special handling. The liquid chocolate is transported in high temperature tanker trailers directly to the candy factories, where it is poured into immediate candy production.

PRODUCTION AND DISTRIBUTION

When we walk down the aisle of our supermarket, we find a great variety of all kinds of foods. In the frozen foods section we find anything that is grown in any season. Products have been quick frozen and shipped by refrigerated or "reefer" trucks from great distances to our local market.

Little more than twenty years ago the frozen foods section was a very small counter, supplying ice cream and local food products.

The frozen food industry of today has been made possible by the development of refrigerated truck carriers. "Reefer" trucks carry 70% of all frozen foods and have helped this industry to expand into a four billion dollar yearly business.

In the early years of development, frozen foods were shipped by the railroads, using ice refrigeration. Temperatures were not low enough and shipment was not satisfactory.

The trucking industry pioneered the development of mechanical refrigeration. Refrigerator trucks solved the problem of transporting perishables. Railroads followed with refrigerator cars.

Our supermarkets depend on the refrigerator truck to keep the frozen foods section stocked. Trucking has made the growth and expansion of this industry possible.

Without the refrigerator truck, distribution of the product would be limited. Trucking has made the frozen food industry into big business and has brought a greater variety to our selection of foods.

The trucking industry serves the needs of our nation in many ways. It provides fast, specialized service. It is the most convenient and flexible of all forms of transportation. Trucking cuts costs in packaging and crating. Trucks provide door to door shipment, handling the whole job.

Our nation is economically dependent upon truck transportation. The trucking industry has helped to make our way of life a better one.

PICTURE CREDITS

Front Cover: Lou Jacobs Jr.
Page 3: Lou Jacobs Jr.
Page 4: North American Van Lines
Page 7: American Trucking Association
Page 8: Lou Jacobs Jr.
Page 9: United States Dept. of Agriculture
Page 10: Lou Jacobs Jr.
Page 12: Freightliner
Page 13: Lou Jacobs Jr.
Page 15: Lou Jacobs Jr.
Page 16: Union Pacific Railroad
Page 18: Sea-Land Service, Inc.
Page 19: Santa Fe Railway
Page 21: Port of Los Angeles
Page 23: North American Van Lines
Page 24: U.S. Borax
Page 26: General Motors
Page 27: General Motors
Page 29: Pan American World Airways
Page 31: Lou Jacobs Jr.
Page 32: Transcon Lines
Page 34: California Highway Patrol
Page 35: Transcon Lines
Page 36: Pacific Intermountain Express
Page 37: Lou Jacobs Jr.
Page 38: Consolidated Freightways
Page 39: Lou Jacobs
Page 40: Transcon Lines
Page 42: Freightliner
Page 43: Jon Madian
Page 44: Lou Jacobs Jr.
Page 45: Helen Brush—T.B. & Resp. Disease Assn.
of Los Angeles County

Page 46: Lou Jacobs Jr.
Page 48: Freightliner
Page 49: Lou Jacobs Jr.
Page 50: Freightliner
Page 51: Lou Jacobs
Page 52: Lou Jacobs Jr.
Page 53: North American Van Lines
Page 54: Freightliner
Page 55: North American Van Lines
Page 56: Transcon Lines
Page 58: Transcon Lines
Page 59: Lou Jacobs
Page 60: Consolidated Freightways
Page 61: Consolidated Freightways
Page 62: Transcon Lines
Page 63: Consolidated Freightways
Page 64: Transcon Lines
Page 65: Transcon Lines
Page 66: Pacific Intermountain Express
Page 67: Transcon Lines
Page 68: Transcon Lines
Page 69: Consolidated Freightways
Page 71: Consolidated Freightways
Page 72: Lou Jacobs Jr.
Page 73: Lou Jacobs Jr.
Page 74: North American Rockwell Corp.
Page 77: Lou Jacobs Jr.
Page 79: Go Magazine